In God's Right Hand

WHOM SHALL I FEAR?

Michelle J. Goff

Iron Rose Sister Ministries

Michelle J. Goff / CreateSpace
Iron Rose Sister Ministries
www.IronRoseSister.com
1-501-593-4849

Book Layout ©2013 BookDesignTemplates.com

In God's Right Hand / Michelle J. Goff.—1st ed.
ISBN 978-0-9963602-0-3 (sc)
ISBN 978-0-9963602-1-0 (e)

Contents

*To my friends and family who have been at my right hand
in support, and have encouraged me to remain in
God's right hand when my spirit is weak or I forget
the strength and blessings available to me there.*

Acknowledgements

Reflecting on all those who have made this second book possible is a humbling experience. God is a faithful provider and he has made this book a reality by carrying me in his right hand. My primary thanks go to my loving heavenly Father.

Secondly, Katie Forbess, you are my right-hand woman in all things Iron Rose Sister Ministries—way more than a glorified cheerleader! Deep and sincere thanks, my friend.

My parents have always been a support at my right hand, no matter what the endeavor, and this book is no exception. For that, and many other things, I thank you both.

Also, great appreciation goes to Jennifer (Goff) Sale for sisterly edits, comments, and suggestions, starting on our spiritual birthday, which made our collaboration all the more special.

Special recognition also goes to the women at the Northwest Church of Christ in Denver, Colorado, for being the pilot group for this study.

Additional editing thanks go to George Brown, Teresa Sosebee, and Christa Duve.

I have not faced any aspect of this process alone. Huge thanks to the following specific individuals for their assistance:

- Susan Tolleson for her editing skills and encouragement through Propel Book Coaching.
- Cynthia Cedeño for facilitating a writing retreat to knock out a first draft of the first five chapters.
- Leslie Dean Photography for the cover image.
- Allan Javellana, our hand model, for the front cover.
- Kenneth Mills for the cover design.
- Greg Douglas for the bio picture.
- Joel Friedlander, Book Template Designs.

Iron Rose Sister Ministries
Bible Studies Format

The Iron Rose Sister Ministries (IRSM) Bible Studies are designed for a small-group context. Even if it were possible for me to give you "all the answers" and share my perspective on the verses and concepts being presented, I cannot emphasize enough the value of fellowship, discussion, and prayer with other Christian sisters! The format of the IRSM Bible Studies allows for greater discussion, depth of insight, and unique perspectives. If you don't follow the book exactly, that's okay! I invite you to make the studies your own, to allow the Spirit to lead, and to treat the studies as a guide and a resource, not a formula.

The IRSM Bible Studies also provide the opportunity for spiritual journaling on a personal level. I encourage you to date the chapters and add notes in the margins in addition to answering the questions. The "Common Threads" will also allow you to chronicle your personal growth individually and in communion with other women in your small group, your Iron Rose Sisters.

Using the image of the rose and the IRSM logo, the bloom of the rose represents areas in which we long to grow. Through these studies, we can also identify thorns we'd like to work on removing or need help to remove. They may be thorns like Paul's (2 Cor. 12:7-10), but by identifying them, we can know where they are and either dull them or stop sticking ourselves and others with them. The final Common Thread is the iron, which is best defined and facilitated in communion with other Christian sisters, Iron Rose Sisters.

Common Threads in IRSM Studies

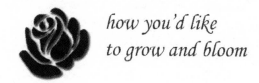

*how you'd like
to grow and bloom*

*a thorn you'd
like to remove*

*an area in which you are striving
to dig deeper or need to have
someone hold you accountable*

What is an Iron Rose Sister?

An Iron Rose Sister is a Christian sister who serves as iron sharpening iron (Prov. 27:17), encouraging and inspiring others to be as beautiful as a rose in spite of a few thorns.

Purposes of Iron Rose Sister relationships:

Encouragement and inspiration

Prayer

Understanding and affirmation

Confidentiality

Spiritual audit (IRS)

Mutual call to holy living

Spiritual friendship and conversation

Recommendations for Iron Rose Sister Ministries Bible Studies:

- Allow for at least a 90-minute meeting time weekly.
    - We're women – we like to talk!
    - Prayer time
    - Depth of conversation and discussion
- Rotate leading the discussion among EACH of the women.
    - Everyone can lead!
    - Everyone will grow!
    - For additional suggestions, see the Leader's Guide (pg. 7)
- Commit to reading the chapter ahead of time.
    - The discussion will be richer and deeper if everyone comes prepared.
    - How much you put in will be directly proportional to how much you get out.
    - You will need to do these studies with your favorite Bible in hand.
    - All verses, unless otherwise noted, are quoted from the New International Version.
- Follow up with each other during the week.
    - Prayer
    - Encouragement
    - Common Threads

 The IRSM logo designation is used to highlight questions that lend themselves to good group discussion: ice-breakers, questions for depth of insight or additional perspectives, and areas for growth and sharing.

Leader's Guide

As presented in the *Iron Rose Sister Ministries Bible Studies Format*, the group is encouraged to rotate who leads the discussion each week.

Even if you do not feel equipped to lead or feel that you lack adequate experience to do so, it is a rich opportunity for growth and blessing. You are among sisters and friends that are supporting you in this part of your journey, as well.

Tips or reminders, especially for new leaders:

- Make it your own and allow the Spirit to lead—these studies are a resource, not a script.
    - Select which questions you would like to discuss, and plan for ones you might need to skip if you are running short on time.
    - You are welcome to add questions of your own or highlight portions of the chapter that most stood out to you, whether they were designated for discussion or not.
- Leading is about facilitating the discussion, not about having all the answers.
    - When someone brings up a difficult situation or challenging question, you can always open it up to the group for answers from Scripture, not just personal advice.
    - The answer may merit further study of Scripture or the consultation of someone with more experience in the

Word and/or experience regarding that type of situation. That's okay! We're digging deeper.

- Be willing to answer the designated discussion questions first, using your own examples, but avoid the temptation to do all the talking.
  - ○ Allow for awkward silence in order to provide the opportunity for others to share.
  - ○ It's okay to call on someone and encourage them to answer a specific question.
  - ○ "Why or why not?" are good follow-up questions for discussion.
- Include additional examples from Scripture and encourage others to do the same.
  - ○ Online Bible programs such as BibleGateway.com provide excellent resources like multiple versions of the Bible, concordances (to look up the occurrences of a word), Bible dictionaries, and commentaries.
- Give a practical wrap-up conclusion or "take-home" application from the week as you close with the Common Threads.
- Be sure to budget some time for prayer.
- Remember our purposes as students of the Word and daughters of the King. We are striving to deepen our relationships with God and one another—to be Iron Rose Sisters that serve as iron sharpening iron as we encourage and inspire one another to be as beautiful as a rose in spite of a few thorns.

Introduction

While debating what car to purchase, I had all but settled on a Toyota® Corolla. As I weighed the merits of my choice and finalized my decision, the other Corollas on the road began to jump out at me. I'm sure they had been there all along, but my awareness was heightened by my attentiveness to my new car.

In a similar fashion, my fascination with the reference to God's right hand began while I was meditating on Isaiah 41 at a ladies' retreat hosted by the South Baton Rouge Church of Christ in September 2012. I later included those reflections in an article for *Wineskins* magazine (May 2013), and in chapter 4 of the first Iron Rose Sister Ministries interactive Bible study, *Human AND Holy*. I will share some of those reflections in Chapter 2: A Promise of Protection and Salvation.

However, after that weekend, like my Corolla, I started to notice how often the Bible refers to God's right hand: sixty-four times, according to the NIV! The references were jumping off of the pages of Scripture and I was captivated. It was as if God's right hand was guiding me to those passages and, ultimately, to sharing the encouragement found through those verses with you.

When facing challenges, filled with fear, or on shaky ground, I have been renewed and strengthened by the reminder that I am secure in God's right hand.

Please join me in taking God's right hand as he enlightens us and broadens our understanding of the honor, blessing, power, authority, protection, salvation, strength, and righteousness that come at his right hand.

CHAPTER 1

A Place of Honor and Blessing

My childlike knowledge of God has grown over the years. Sunday-school class introduced me to the God of Noah, David, and Joseph. I loved those stories and the adventures they represented.

But as I have gotten older, I have come to realize that the Creator of the heavens and the earth is also the author of my life. My understanding of God has matured as I have come to know him personally, not just *about* him, through Bible stories.

The same God who saved Noah and his family in the ark (Gen. 6) is the God who has the power to save me from this destructive world. Therefore, I have hope (Lam. 3:21).

God accompanied David to kill Goliath (1 Sam. 17), and he walks with me today to slay my personal giants. Whom shall I fear? (Ps. 27:1)

Joseph's brothers threw him in a pit, sold him into slavery, deceived their father, and were basically jerks to their younger brother out of jealousy. But the same God who rescued Joseph and redeemed his story is the God who works to bring all things to good for those that love him (Gen. 50:20; Rom. 8:28). I can trust him and his plan (Prov. 3:5-6).

One of the most revealing and enlightening aspects of God's character I have come to rely on and trust is his right hand. For me, it has become a place of peace and security. When I am frustrated, discouraged, confused, broken—no matter what I am facing—I can rest secure in God's right hand.

It is my prayer that you come to *know* God—not just know about him—through this study of his right hand. May you, too, rest in the security his right hand provides, knowing and trusting the promises obtainable at his right hand.

We will explore his right hand as a promise of protection and salvation, a demonstration of power and authority, a source of strength, a standard of righteousness, and where Jesus sits to intercede for us.

But why God's right hand?

The Significance of the Right Hand

Which hand goes over your heart when you recite the pledge of allegiance?

You are called to testify in court. What hand do they ask you to raise as you swear to tell the truth, the whole truth, and nothing but the truth?

According to more than a dozen sources, from seventy to ninety percent of the population worldwide is right-handed. And most of our world is ordered with that bent. Scissors, a handshake, notebooks, and school desks—all are designed to accommodate the right-handed majority of the population.

One of my best friends and her husband are both left-handed. When I am cooking in their kitchen, lost and in search of something, we joke that I have to think like a left-handed person in order to locate the desired utensil or cookware. Nine times out of ten, that brief adjustment in my thinking allows me to immediately locate the item I was hunting.

My maternal grandfather is left-handed, but when he was in elementary school, the teacher bound his left hand so that he would be forced to learn to write with his right. He is now ambidextrous in many of the things he does, but his left-hand dominance favored him greatly on the basketball court. No one was expecting that left-handed jump shot!

Neither did anyone see Ehud coming when he used his left hand to thrust his sword into the obese belly of Eglon, king of Moab (Judg. 3). Some scholars suggest that Ehud's left-handedness was indicative of an underhanded or deceitful nature, often associated with the few who had left-handed predominance during Bible times.

While the stigma attached to left-handed people has diminished in recent decades, the significance of the right hand is echoed and favored in Scripture, starting in Genesis with familial blessings.

Turn to Genesis 48 and let's read the entire chapter. Make a list of the characters in this chapter and explain how they are related to each other, making special note of birth order.

How did Joseph line up his sons for Jacob's blessing?

What did Jacob (Israel) do instead?

What insight do we gain about the significance of the right hand for blessings?

God's Right Hand

According to the NIV, we see a direct reference to God's right hand sixty-four times in the Old and New Testament (listed in Appendix A). Before we delve into a more in-depth description of the various facets of his right hand in subsequent chapters, let's look at a few of those blessings in the Psalms.

Describe the blessing that comes at God's right hand in the following psalms:

Psalm 17:6-9

Psalm 18:30-36

Psalm 20

Psalm 44:1-3

Psalm 48:10

Psalm 110:1

Which of these characteristics of God's right hand is most encouraging to you? Why?

The place of honor at God's right hand implies relationship, not just a blessing at a distance. We are invited to be a daughter of the King with all the rights and privileges that come from being a child of God. I, Michelle, am a daughter of the King, not just a member of his kingdom.

Say that with me, inserting your own name: "**I, _____, am a daughter of the King, not just a member of his kingdom.**"

 What is the significance of that statement for you personally?

God chooses to adopt us, bless us, and afford us a place of honor at his right hand!

 What do the verses on the following page highlight about being a child of God?

Romans 8:15-17

Galatians 4:4-7

Ephesians 1:4-6

John 1:12-13

1 John 3:1-2

God's love for his children provides the assurance of privilege and security for the members of his family. The security and stability we are promised as a child of God is in direct contrast to the broken homes in which many grew up.

True security cannot be found in man, but we can know genuine security in God's right hand. There is "abiding security [for] true children of God" (Packer, *Knowing God*, pg. 209).

Abiding security removes the fear. When I am secure in God's right hand, whom shall I fear?

Secure in God's Right Hand

Fear is the opposite of security, which is what God generously offers his beloved children. He extends his right hand in invitation of blessing and guidance, protection and peace, strength and promise.

As women, we deeply long for security. According to *His Needs, Her Needs* by William F. Harley Jr., men and women each have five basic emotional needs. Security is the underlying common element of the top five emotional needs that women have (affection, conversation, honesty and openness, financial support, and family commitment). While Harley's book focuses on the relationship between husband and wife, emotional, financial, and even physical security are important to every woman.

Why do you think so many women are attracted to a man in uniform? He's the superhero ready to come in and save the day; the prince charming who rides in on the white horse; the fireman who's ready for his task to rescue us from a burning building. If we know someone is there to protect us, we no longer allow the fear of our circumstances to consume us.

Fear steals our joy. Security brings peace. Fear leads to chaos and overwhelmed feelings of loneliness. Security in God's right hand keeps us centered and reminds us we are not alone. Fear clouds our judgment. Security in God's right hand guides us in paths of righteousness.

Whom shall I fear? No one and no thing if I am firmly planted in God's right hand!

Can we fully grasp what God offers in his right hand if our own fist is clenched?

The author of this story is unknown, but this often-used illustration is an excellent example of what God has waiting for us when we unclench our fists and grasp his right hand.

The Pearl Necklace: A Father's Blessing

The cheerful girl with bouncy golden curls was almost five. Waiting with her mother at the checkout stand, she saw them: a circle of glistening white pearls in a pink foil box. "Oh please, mommy. Can I have them? Please, mommy, please?"

Quickly the mother checked the back of the little foil box and then looked back into the pleading blue eyes of her daughter's upturned face. "They're $1.95. That's almost $2.00. If you really want them, I'll think of some extra chores for you, and in no time, you can save enough money to buy them for yourself. Your birthday's only a week away and you might get another crisp dollar bill from grandma, as well."

As soon as Jenny got home, she emptied her penny bank and counted out seventeen pennies. After dinner, she did more than her share of chores, then went to the neighbor and asked Mrs. McJames if she could pick dandelions for ten cents. On her birthday, grandma gave her another new dollar bill, and at last she had enough money to buy the necklace.

Jenny loved her pearls. They made her feel dressed up and grown up. She wore them everywhere—Sunday school, kindergarten, even to bed. The only time she took them off was when she went swimming or had a bubble bath. Mother said if they got wet, they might turn her neck green.

Jenny had a very loving daddy, and every night when she was ready for bed, he would stop whatever he was doing and come upstairs to read her a story. One night when he finished the story, he asked Jenny, "Do you love me?"

"Oh yes, daddy. You know that I love you."

"Then give me your pearls."

"Oh, daddy, not my pearls. But you can have Princess—the white horse from my collection—the one with the pink tail. Remember, daddy? The one you gave me. She's my favorite."

"That's okay, honey. Daddy loves you. Good night." And he brushed her cheek with a kiss.

About a week later, after her bedtime story, Jenny's daddy asked again, "Do you love me?"

"Daddy, you know I love you."

"Then give me your pearls."

"Oh daddy, not my pearls. But you can have my baby doll—the brand new one I got for my birthday. She is so beautiful and you can have the yellow blanket that matches her sleeper."

"That's okay. Sleep well. God bless you, little one. Daddy loves you." And as always, he brushed her cheek with a gentle kiss.

A few nights later when her daddy came in, Jenny was sitting on her bed with her legs crossed Indian-style. As he came close, he noticed her chin was trembling and one silent tear rolled down her cheek.

"What is it, Jenny? What's the matter?"

Jenny didn't say anything but lifted her tiny hand up to her daddy. And when she opened it, there was her pearl necklace. With a little quiver, she finally said, "Here, daddy. It's for you."

With tears gathering in his own eyes, Jenny's kind daddy reached out with one hand to take the dime-store necklace, and with the other hand he reached into his pocket and pulled out a blue velvet case with a strand of genuine pearls and gave them to Jenny. He had had them all the time. He was just waiting for her to give up the dime-store stuff so he could give her the genuine treasure.

So it is with our heavenly Father. He is waiting for us to give up the cheap things in our lives so that he can bless us with beautiful treasure.

What God offers is greater than a real pearl necklace for his daughter. He invites us to a place of honor at his right hand. As an adopted daughter of the King, he showers us with blessings that pour from his right hand. But we cannot grasp his hand and accept those blessings if we don't first relinquish whatever we are clinging to with clenched fists.

"Dear God,

I am so afraid to open my clenched fists!

Who will I be when I have nothing left to hold on to?

Who will I be when I stand before you with empty hands?

Please help me to gradually open my hands

and to discover that I am not what I own. but what you want to give me."

— Henri J.M. Nouwen, *The Only Necessary Thing: Living a Prayerful Life*, pg. 206

 Reflection: What are you clinging to with clenched fists? What do you need to surrender in order to embrace God's promises and grasp his right hand?

The answer to the reflection question is a perfect segue for the Common Threads.

The Common Threads help make the lesson personal and practical. Its elements are taken from the three parts of the Iron Rose Sister Ministries (IRSM) logo. In light of the primary goal of IRSM—to equip women to connect to God and one another more deeply—I encourage you to be honest, sharing your responses in prayer with the other women in your group, your Iron Rose Sisters.

Common Threads:

 An area in which you'd like to grow or bloom.

A thorn you'd like to remove.

_____

_____

An area in which you'd like to dig deeper or need someone to hold you accountable.

_____

_____

A message of hope, an encouraging word, or scripture.

_____

_____

CHAPTER 2

A Promise of Protection and Salvation

round the age of six, I had a dark pink shirt with black lettering across the chest that said "Princess." I wore the shirt with all the pride that comes with that title. After outgrowing the shirt and passing it on to my three younger sisters, I remember wanting it back for the special way I felt when I wore it. "Princess." It was as if no one else but me was a princess that day, and the shirt afforded protection from anyone who thought otherwise.

When we are clothed with Christ (Gal. 3:27), we are privileged to share in the same kind of protection from Satan's attacks. We are enveloped in the special feeling that comes from being a daughter of the King.

When you look in the mirror today, picture yourself wearing a princess shirt that has been lovingly placed on your shoulders. You are a beloved daughter of the King, his princess!

God loves each of his daughters with an everlasting love (Jer. 31:3). He longs to protect his precious princesses and calm our fears.

Read Isaiah 43:1-7. What reasons does God give to not fear?

Did you catch the personal promise in the first verse? "Do not fear, for I have redeemed you. I have called you by name; you are mine" (Isa. 43:1b).

Copy below the above portion of verse 1. As you write it out, add your name where it says "you," and imagine God comforting you and assuring you as he speaks these words over you.

God knows each of his daughters intimately. He calls us by name. He knows the number of hairs on our head. And lest you think the promises in Isaiah 43 were only for Jacob, what does Matthew 10:29-31 say you are worth?

Do Not Fear at God's Right Hand

The admonition, "do not fear," from Isaiah 43 is echoed in Isaiah 41. Read verses 8-14 and list the different ways in which the concept of "do not fear" is expressed. (Hint: They all start with "do not.")

Why do you think God wanted Isaiah to share this admonition several times in various ways?

 On the flip side, we are given promises in those same verses, assurances that give us the strength not to succumb to fear. List the promises presented in those same verses.

Which is the specific promise at God's right hand in verse 10?

My own study of these verses in Isaiah 41 was the initial inspiration for this book, and a deeper look at God's right hand. Allow me to walk you through some of my reflections and the circumstances surrounding that time.

My Own Journey into God's Right Hand

I have always clung to God's promises in Joshua 1:5 that he will never leave us nor forsake us; his call to be strong and courageous and not be afraid in verses 6, 7, and 9; and his promise to always be with us at the end of verse 9. Did you recognize the similar language of promise and accompaniment in Isaiah 41:10? They are parallel passages. However, Isaiah adds a unique detail—these promises come at God's right hand.

I began to glimpse the picture of embrace that God paints of his right hand in verses 10 and 13, but had never fully grasped its beauty and powerful comfort until a moment when I truly needed it.

It was a broken time in my life. And that is an understatement. My fiancé had suddenly and unexpectedly ended our relationship two-and-a-half months before the wedding. I was in shock and depressed—so depressed that I was scaring my friends and family. I began having social anxiety, including a few panic attacks. I was overwhelmed by a myriad of emotions and reactions that were totally foreign to me.

At a loss of what to do, a friend invited me to spend a few days at her house in Atlanta (I was living in Baton Rouge, Louisiana, at the time). We would then drive to the South Baton Rouge Church of Christ ladies' retreat on the Alabama coast, and I would return with friends to Baton Rouge after the retreat.

Numb and unable to make my own decisions, I agreed. Fast forward to three weeks after the breakup, at the ladies retreat I would've preferred to skip. In an effort to avoid conversation and looks of pity from the other women present, I evaded eye contact altogether and buried my face in my Bible. I found myself reading and meditating on Isaiah 41.

I noticed the promise in verse 10 that God "will uphold you in [his] righteous right hand." Then, in verse 13, I read that God takes hold of "your right hand and says to you, Do not fear; I will help you." *His* right hand with *your* right hand. Both people have to be facing each other to engage their right hands.

What a realization: God, facing me, seeing my pain, taking my hand and holding me in his embrace. Wow. The God of all comfort bathed me with comfort in his loving presence at that moment, meeting me where I was and leading me toward healing.

Before we continue, I invite you to take a moment and taste that promise. Turn to each of the women in your small group, an Iron Rose Sister, look her in the eyes and grasp her right hand as you speak the following words of truth: "God is holding you in his right hand."

What impact do those words have when spoken over you? (You may want to take advantage of the Notes pages in the back of the book or in your own notebook to journal what it means for God to hold you in his right hand.)

For me, it was life changing. The moment on that Saturday afternoon in September when I felt God's right hand of protection and comfort is forever etched in my brain and my heart. It was a pivotal moment in which God saw me, broken and naked before him, and that was okay. He welcomed me into his arms, and I think it was the first time I truly took a cleansing breath since the wind had been knocked out of me three weeks before.

Staying in God's Right Hand

Over the next few weeks, months, and years, I continued to cling to the memory and the promise of the security I had found in God's right hand. My fears did not immediately go away, but I was reminded that I could trust the One who is faithful—the One who had extended his right hand to save me and would do so time and time again.

I feared future attacks when I was overcome by doubt and frustration, but I trusted in the One who protects, and I depended on the promise that he holds me in his right hand. I rested, comforted in that promise, and allowed myself to just spend some time hanging out in God's right hand—secure and at peace.

My place in God's right hand did not change my circumstances, but it reminded me that I *can* always trust in the God who is bigger than any circumstance! Furthermore, his right hand is big enough to hold you, too!

> *Suffering invites us to place our hurts in larger hands. In Christ we see God suffering—for us. And calling us to share in God's suffering love for a hurting world. The small and even overpowering pains of our lives are intimately connected with the greater pains of Christ. Our daily sorrows are anchored in a greater sorrow and therefore a larger hope.* — Henri J.M. Nouwen

I placed my burdens, my pain, and my sorrow in God's capable hands. God's right hand carried me through counseling, along with the support of friends and family. God's right hand led me to take one step at a time and share my struggles and the comfort I had received with others so that none of us would feel alone (2 Cor. 1:3-7). God's right hand led me to launch Iron Rose Sister Ministries and share words of hope and promise in English and Spanish to women across the Americas.

"By his wounds, we are healed" (Isa. 53:5). The generous gift of salvation was at the expense of his pierced right hand for those who die with him to be raised in newness of life (Rom. 6:1-6).

 Take a moment and let that sink in. What is the cost of God's protection and salvation?

We find God's promise of protection and salvation in his right hand in the following three verses. What else do these verses have in common?

Psalm 17:7

Psalm 44:3

Psalm 108:6

What is the protection and salvation at God's right hand an extension of?

Prayer Keeps Us in God's Right Hand

Does God really love me that much? Yes! Satan wants to fill us with feelings of unworthiness. And when God's love fades from my awareness, when Satan's assaults are fierce, I can always go to the Father in prayer—it keeps me present and secure in his right hand.

Prayer is one of the best tools we have in our arsenal to fight against Satan's attacks and combat the doubts that enhance our fears. Prayer is not merely going to God with our requests. It is two-way communication with our heavenly Father: listening to his promises and laying at his feet the burdens of our heart.

Through prayer, we remain connected in relationship with God. No relationship will have any depth or endure the test of time if there is not healthy and constant communication. The more we connect with the Father through prayer, the more we get to know him and are reminded of his promises, and the easier it is to remain in his right hand.

One of the best prayer warrior examples in the Bible is Daniel. We see his trust in God and God's plan through various points in his life. What was his commitment to prayer? (Dan. 6:10-11)

Whether or not you are familiar with the story, go back and read all of Daniel 6. It's not just a children's story. There are powerful applications for us as women today. What did God's angel do in Daniel 6:22?

If God can shut the mouths of ferocious lions, what else can he do to protect and save us from certain destruction? What or whom shall we fear?

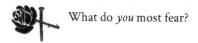 What do *you* most fear?

Daniel's relationship with God put his fears into perspective. Daniel called on the name of the Lord in submission and obedience, no matter what the outcome. His friends—Shadrach, Meshach, and Abednego—did the same in Daniel 3 when they were threatened with death in a fiery furnace.

"If we are thrown into the blazing furnace, the God we serve is able to save us from it, and he will rescue us from your hand, O king. But even if he does not, we want you to know, O king, that we will not serve your gods or worship the image of gold you have set up" (Dan. 3:17-18).

Both King Nebuchadnezzar and King Darius changed their tune after seeing God's protection and salvation for his people—those who were called by his name.

The night before he went to the cross, Jesus prayed for our protection (John 17:11-19). By what power does he say we will be protected?

Victory in God's Right Hand

Jesus, Daniel, and David each remind us that there is power when we call upon the name of the Lord. Psalm 20 highlights the protection received by the name of the Lord our God and also reminds us that we can trust in the saving power of God's right hand (verse 6).

Join me in reading David's prayer in Psalm 20 (written out below). When you read through it the first time, circle the references to the name of God, and put a star by any reference to God's right hand.

The second time you read it, read it as if David is praying this specifically over you.

May the Lord answer you when you are in distress;
  may the name of the God of Jacob protect you.
May he send you help from the sanctuary
  and grant you support from Zion.
May he remember all your sacrifices
  and accept your burnt offerings.
May he give you the desire of your heart
  and make all your plans succeed.
May we shout for joy over your victory
  and lift up our banners in the name of our God.
May the Lord grant all your requests.

Now this I know:
  The Lord gives victory to his anointed.
He answers him from his heavenly sanctuary
  with the victorious power of his right hand.
Some trust in chariots and some in horses,
  but we trust in the name of the Lord our God.
They are brought to their knees and fall,
  but we rise up and stand firm.

(cont'd on next page)

Lord, give victory to the king!
Answer us when we call!

 What kind of transition does David go through from the start to the end of this psalm?

As you can imagine from the story I recounted earlier in this chapter, many cries of distress escaped my lips, but just like David in verse 5, we can now shout for joy over that victory and raise a banner in the name of our God!

In the banner on the following page, make note of a victory you can rejoice over with the women in your small group. God has provided these women as Iron Rose Sisters: to be like iron sharpening iron and to encourage and inspire you to be as beautiful as a rose, in spite of a few thorns. They are there to rejoice when you rejoice and mourn when you mourn (Rom. 12:15). Let's put that into practice now!

Victory Banner

What can be celebrated now in victory may have seemed like an impossibility in the early stages of despair. Even after finding protection in God's right hand, which is what impassioned and inspired me to write this book, it was a process to learn to trust again.

God knows the trepidation with which we hesitate to trust after we have been hurt, and he meets us there. It can be difficult to trust someone else to protect us. Nevertheless, the security we find in God's protection is on a whole different level. Whom shall I fear? "If God is for me, who can be against me?" (Rom. 8:31). "We trust in the name of the Lord our God!" (Ps. 20:6)

We will continue to explore the various facets of God's right hand as referenced in Scripture, but as we close, I invite you to embrace in your life the promise of protection and salvation at God's right hand. Let's make this very personal and practical through a time of prayer and reflection with the Common Threads.

Common Threads:

An area in which you'd like to grow or bloom.

_____

_____

A thorn you'd like to remove.

_____

_____

An area in which you'd like to dig deeper or need someone to hold you accountable.

_____

_____

A message of hope, an encouraging word, or scripture.

_____

_____

CHAPTER 3

A Demonstration of Power and Authority

"Phenomenal cosmic power! Itty bitty living space." That is one of my favorite quotes from the Disney movie *Aladdin*. The genie describes his powers and bemoans his limitations to Aladdin as he explains in song the intricacies of the three wishes he is now there to grant.

Sometimes we treat God like a cosmic genie, presenting our wishes in prayer, but limiting him to a golden lamp, a restrictive box that restrains his true power and authority in our lives.

God's right hand is infinitely powerful and has ultimate authority. Whether or not we relinquish the little power and authority we have over our own lives through free will, God is the one in control.

The King of kings is our Father who invites us to sit at his right hand—a place of honor and blessing. But as the King, he is also in a position of power and authority.

List five things God's power has done using examples from Scripture. Be sure to include the biblical reference. Star your favorite example.

We serve a powerful God! Amen? God is the same yesterday, today, and forever (Heb. 13:8), but we forget that truth when our hearts fill with fear and our souls with doubt. We lose sight of the demonstrations of his power and authority when the chaos of life clouds our vision.

What does Asaph say he will remember in Psalm 77:10-12?

Let's take a moment to remember a few more specific demonstrations of power and authority at God's right hand. According to the following verses, what was done by God's right hand?

Exodus 15:6, 12

Psalm 45:4

Isaiah 48:13

How does God display that power today? Or does he?

List three things God's power has done in your life.

When I doubt God's power in my life, one of my go-to verses to remind me of his power is Ephesians 3:20-21:

Now to him who is able to do immeasurably more than all we ask or imagine, according to his power that is at work within us, to him be glory in the church and in Christ Jesus throughout all generations, for ever and ever! Amen.

Underline where it says that God's power is at work. Is there anything impossible with God?

 Why does it sometimes feel like that power is not at work within us?

 Which is easier to allow to work in your life: God's power or his authority? What is the difference between the two?

Leaving the Power *and* the Authority in God's Right Hand

Access to God's power in my life? Yes, please! But in order to give him that power, I have to leave him in charge and follow his wisdom and authority? Um, let me think about that... We are not the only ones that have struggled to surrender to God and submit to his authority.

Whose right arm did God strengthen in Isaiah 63:12?

What did God give his servant's right hand power to do?

God strengthens our right hand, but we must remember who is the ultimate source of power and authority.

Isaiah references the events of Exodus 14. Turn with me to Exodus 14 to highlight one more aspect of the story.

What did the Israelites fear in Exodus 14:10-12?

How does Moses respond in verses 13-14?

Write out Exodus 14:14 below.

 God's got this! Whatever you fear, God will fight for you. You need only to be still. What happens when we go rogue and think we can do it on our own—when we fail to recognize God's authority?

Moses wanted to do it his own way, forgetting that his power came from God and that it was only by God's authority that he could perform the miracles he had done in leading the Israelite nation. Let's look at the story in Numbers 20:1-13. What did God ask Moses to do to provide for the people?

What did Moses do instead?

We are assured a destructive path if we do not submit to God's authority. Allow me to share an illustration of God's authority in comparison with ours.

The captain on the bridge of a large naval vessel saw a light ahead on a collision course. He signaled, "Alter your course ten degrees south."

The reply came back, "Alter your course ten degrees north."

The captain then signaled, "Alter your course ten degrees south. I am a captain."

The reply: "Alter your course ten degrees north. I am a seaman third-class."

The furious captain signaled, "Alter your course ten degrees south. I am a battle-ship."

The reply: "Alter your course ten degrees north. I am a lighthouse."

God's authority is definitive, absolute, and uncompromising. In Matthew 27:27-31, the soldiers made a mockery of Jesus' power and authority by putting a robe on his back, a crown of thorns on his head, and a staff in his right hand.

Do we make a mockery of Christ's power and authority today? How so or how do we not?

Another way of expressing the concepts of power and authority is control. Control is an elusive intangible that always seems to be outside of my grasp. Maybe because I need to leave it in the right hand of the one who truly has it all under control.

In launching Iron Rose Sister Ministries, I stepped out in faith. I quit my job in local full-time ministry to focus on a more global ministry. I sold my house and moved across the country into my third sister and brother-in-law's basement. (I thank them for their generous hospitality.) All of the things that I had previously thought were under my control, I was forced to surrender in submission to God's will.

By inviting God to take control of my life, I was asking him to demonstrate the same power and authority that he exercises in the Bible. Actually, to say that I invited him to take complete control may be a bit of a stretch. I've been known to have a few control issues.

It's All Part of the Journey

Driven. Type-A personality. Stubborn. Extremely organized. Control freak. I've heard it all. And God has had to polish a number of rough edges to soften my demeanor and interactions with others.

This lesson never became more real than it did on a day trip to the beach with a group of Venezuelans. While serving as a missionary in Latin America, flexibility needs to be your middle name. Plans are made, but schedules are merely a suggestion.

The East Caracas congregation that started meeting in my apartment in February 2003 was taking a trip to the beach for a relaxing holiday. Yet some of us were far from relaxed. Okay, *I* was far from relaxed.

We were supposed to meet at 6:30 a.m. to caravan with a bus and a few vehicles, including my Jeep® Grand Cherokee. Never the morning person, I was willing to sacrifice for my Christian brothers and sisters, as well as a visit to the clear waters of the Caribbean. The beach was calling me and I was ready to go.

The minutes ticked by...6:45, 7:00, 7:15, 7:30... More than an hour passed since our scheduled departure time, with maybe half of the group there. Anger and frustration started to rise as I bemoaned the sleep I had lost in order to stand on the side of the street waiting for others to arrive before we could depart.

We finally got on the road. It was a less-than-joyous ride for those in my car. My attitude had soured and my patience had worn thin, so silence was my best recourse.

As we got closer to our destination, my temper began to cool, and by the time we reached the boats used to take us over to Caracolito Island Beach, the deep breaths of salty air and the sand between my toes were God's perfect therapy.

Loading the boats was no small feat. If memory serves me correctly, there were about forty of us present for the beach trip, so you can imagine the bags and bags of food, drinks, towels, and other paraphernalia we had carted with us. Finally unloaded on the shore, we began to enjoy ourselves in the waves and in fellowship with other Christians.

A short time later, the admonition to "never kick a volleyball" from one of my camp counselors echoed in my ears. A group of our young men grabbed the volleyball that had been donated from the U.S. and began to use it as a soccer ball across the sand.

My anger, which I thought had subsided from that morning, must have only been held at bay beneath the surface. I felt it bubble over as I calmly and coldly asked for the volleyball back. "You were supposed to bring your own soccer ball. This is a volleyball. You'll ruin it. Thanks for understanding." I vaguely remember mumbling some words to that effect as I returned to the shade and my lunch.

The rest of the day continued uneventfully and we all returned safely to the city, tired, but ready to get cleaned up and go out for the evening. The preacher, his wife, and I had made plans to meet for dinner at a favorite restaurant since none of us would want to cook after a long day at the beach.

Hair still wet from the shower, I grabbed the ringing home phone. I was excited at the prospect of dinner and glad that my day had greatly improved since that morning. I answered with the chipper voice I expected to be reciprocated on the other line.

"Michelle, we're sorry, but we cannot go to dinner with you tonight."

"What? Is something wrong? Did something come up?"

"No, we just really can't be around you. You really hurt and offended us and others with your attitude today. And while we love you, we really just cannot be with you tonight."

Stunned, I stammered an apology and asked what I had done that was so offensive. They did not want to go into specifics with their explanation or the details of the events, but I clearly understood that my attitude had stunk and I had taken out my frustration on others throughout the course of the day.

Before hanging up, I apologized again and they said that they forgave me. "But we still can't go to dinner with you tonight."

"I understand. Thank you."

I immediately dialed the young man who had borrowed the volleyball that afternoon and apologized to him for my attitude and the way in which I had offended him. "I was a poor example of a Christian today and I'm very sorry."

Devastated by my attitude and actions, humbled by the pain I had caused others and the potential damage to our relationships, I spent a long time in prayer and reflection that night and in the days following.

Did I have any control over Venezuelans and their concept of time? No. What power or authority did I have to try and control *any* of the circumstances surrounding that day? None. And in the grand scheme of things, what really mattered: leaving on time, a working volleyball, or a great time of fellowship for a young church?

Realization slowly came over me that "it's all part of the journey." The time of fellowship with the other Christians started when the first of us arrived at the meeting place, continued on the road trip, and blossomed at the beach. It was *all* part of the journey. And I was not in charge of the journey. God was.

I had tried to take things into my own hands and execute my own plan for the day. And I had failed miserably.

Leaving the Control in God's Right Hand

 Whether or not you have control issues to the magnitude of mine, which of the following (listed on the next page) is the biggest hindrance for you in allowing God to be the authority in your life?

- Control issues
- Pride
- Impatience
- Trust
- Other: _____

 Why is it so hard to trust God's power and authority? What is so hard about allowing God to be in control?

There is no right or wrong answer to the two previous questions, but for me personally, my answers could probably be summed up in two words: "surrender" and "fear."

Whom shall I fear?

We will close this chapter's study by looking at David's answer to that question in Psalm 27.

 Why does David say that he doesn't have to fear?

As an echo of Exodus 14:14, write out Psalm 27:14 below.

God's right hand is in control. It is living and active today. We can trust him to fight for us with the same power and authority he has demonstrated throughout time. Our job: Wait, be still, and leave the control in his capable right hand.

"Those who leave everything in God's hand will eventually see God's hand in everything." ~ Anonymous

Common Threads:

An area in which you'd like to grow or bloom.

_____

_____

A thorn you'd like to remove.

_____

_____

An area in which you'd like to dig deeper or need someone to hold you accountable.

_____

_____

A message of hope, an encouraging word, or scripture.

_____

_____

CHAPTER 4

A Source of Strength

Does your family have a favorite movie that you can quote from start to finish? For my family, that movie is *The Princess Bride*, a 1987 film based on a 1973 novel. The witty humor, sarcastic banter, and clever comebacks provide a plethora of quotable quotes. Please indulge me with a couple before drawing from a scene to illustrate a point.

This is the quote that brought my mom to tears of laughter the first time she watched the movie: "Don't pester him. He's had a hard day." (This was stated in reference to Westley after he was revived from a mostly dead state.)

Also from the movie, the to-do list and our answer to one another when we feel overwhelmed or tired: "Tyrone, you know how much I love watching you work, but I've got my country's 500th anniversary to plan, my wedding to arrange, my wife to murder, and Guilder to frame for it; I'm swamped." The response: "Get some rest. If you haven't got your health, you haven't got anything..."

And the fun nightly greeting that makes others uncomfortable when they don't know we are quoting a movie: "Rest well and dream of large women." (What Westley tells the giant after knocking him out.)

I highly recommend the classic fairy tale with a twist. In one scene, the Spaniard Inigo Montoya challenges Westley, dressed as the man in black, to a sword fight. Both men grab their swords with their left hands and deftly maneuver the rocky terrain as they battle. Several minutes into the fight, as Westley is beginning to take the upper hand, he asks his opponent, "Why are you smiling?"

"Because I am not left-handed," is the simple response. Montoya then brandishes his sword in his right hand and attacks him with even greater skill and strength.

Are you smiling at the secret strength you have at your right hand? I am not referring to physical strength or dexterity. Just as God strengthened Moses' right hand to divide the waters to go before them (Isa. 63:12; Ex. 14), God extends those same promises to his children today.

We saw in Isaiah 41 how God takes our right hand in his right hand. Besides the comfort I received by his right hand at the time of the story I shared in chapter 2, there are many other benefits that come when God's right hand meets ours.

 What is the correlation between our right hand and God's right hand in Psalm 16:8-11?

 What encouragement does Psalm 16 give you?

 How does Psalm 121 offer strength to face your fears?

In the Hebrew metaphor, the shade offered at God's right hand represents protection like a shadow from the hot desert sun. What do protection and strength have in common?

The power and protection of God's right hand can strengthen our right hand. Being on God's team is like having the ultimate right-hand man!

Psalm 73:23-26 declares this truth beautifully:

Yet I am always with you;
you hold me by my right hand.
You guide me with your counsel,
and afterward you will take me into glory.
Whom have I in heaven but you?
And earth has nothing I desire besides you.
My flesh and my heart may fail,
but God is the strength of my heart
and my portion forever.

There is strength in knowing that we don't have to go it alone. We can walk hand in hand with the provider of absolute strength.

"Hold My Hand, Aunt M"

We were just getting started on our all-night drive back to Denver. It had been a great weekend visiting grandpa on the farm. I was in the back seat with Kadesh, my nephew who was almost two years old at the time.

Kadesh Austin is named after Grandpa Dean Austin, and it turns out they have more than a name in common.

As we got on the road, I took out the iPad to do some writing, but Kadesh had a better idea. He wanted to hold my hand as he tried to fall asleep. "Hold my hand, Aunt M." Who am I to argue? I closed the iPad and took Kadesh's hand.

We looked at the stars, delighted in the full moon, and pointed out the cars driving by. He soon fell asleep and I returned to my writing, glad I had taken a moment to hold his hand and enjoy the mutual love and relationship between us.

I was reminded of a similar moment sitting on the couch with grandpa that weekend. He had a granddaughter on each side and, while seated there, we grasped each other's hands. We held hands as we prayed before each meal. We grasped hands to help him stand up from the couch. Many special moments were cherished and the strength of family was renewed by taking hold of each other's hands.

My encouragement to you is to take a moment to hold someone's hand—a child, a grandparent, your spouse, a friend... There are many who would greatly appreciate a loving touch, and you will be blessed by making a moment to take their hand.

God invites us to take a moment and grasp his hand each day. During your prayer time today, imagine yourself holding God's hand as you talk with him and listen to him in prayer. Picture yourself in his right hand.

At Rest in God's Right Hand

This was a powerful exercise for me after returning from four years as a missionary in Venezuela. I was suffering from extreme reverse culture shock and had finally taken some time to disconnect from the busyness of life—to pray, rest, walk, and even talk with a counselor to process my re-entry.

During the extended weekend, I mourned the physical distance from my Venezuelan friends, as well as other things I had left behind. After a conversation with the counselor one afternoon, I began to realize the intensity of my emotions and great sense of loss. I knew that I needed to let go of many things I was holding onto from my time in Venezuela if I were to move forward in the new direction God was guiding me.

So after some tearful time in prayer, I pictured myself curled up in God's lap, crying out my pain, warmed by his embrace, and cherished by his right hand stroking my hair.

I garnished strength by his hand and was washed with a peace in his presence. I could almost hear his voice whispering words of comfort and promise in my ear as he brushed my hair aside with his right hand. I fell asleep that night, resting in his presence—a peaceful feeling I treasure to this day.

"On my bed I remember you; I think of you through the watches of the night. Because you are my help, I sing in the shadow of your wings. I cling to you; your right hand upholds me" (Ps. 63:6-8).

I garnered great strength as God's right hand upheld me.

Upheld in God's Right Hand

To uphold means to confirm or support something that has been questioned; to maintain, sustain, preserve, protect, champion, defend, back up; or to stand by.

Which of these definitions describes the way in which you would love for God's right hand to uphold you? Why did you choose that word over the others?

When does God begin to uphold us? When does he stop sustaining us? Let's look to Isaiah 46:3-4 for the answer.

Let's now go back to the Psalms to emphasize the expansive reach of God's right hand to "hold me fast" (Ps. 139:10b). Turn to Psalm 139 and read the entire psalm.

Psalm 139:10a refers to God's hand for guidance—which we will explore in chapter 5—but what other reminders in Psalm 139 can be a source of strength for you?

 Does it comfort you or scare you to know that God knows you so intimately? Why?

The assurances that we cannot go anywhere to escape his presence (Ps. 139) or his love (Rom. 8:35-39) are additional affirmations of

God's right hand to uphold us because the opposite of the verb "uphold" is to "abandon or leave alone."

Do you fear abandonment? Satan wants to convince us that we are alone in those fears and feelings. But even David, a man after God's own heart, struggled with that fear at times. In Psalm 142:4, David cries out to God about feeling alone, with no one at his right hand. He felt abandoned and forgotten.

 In contrast to David's fears, what vivid imagery do we see in Psalm 18:1-3 and 30-36?

 Which image most encourages you to remember that God is our source of strength?

Strengthened at God's Right Hand

Many people tell me I have an excellent memory. It's simply not true. I write everything down, I set reminders in my phone, and I keep things organized so I know where to find what I didn't remember in the first place.

Thankfully, life does not depend on one person's memory. God gives us his Word in order to recollect his promises. God gives us his church so that we can encourage one another and remind each other of truth when our fears threaten to overtake us. We also are strengthened by God's right hand when we join hands with one another.

Solomon lists several advantages of doing things together in Ecclesiastes 4:9-12. Name two of those advantages.

There is strength in the body that cannot be found in a single member (1 Cor. 12:12-27). Each of you has a vital place in the body and no one is more valuable than another.

Our Christian brothers and sisters provide strength, yet may we never forget the ultimate source of strength when we feel weak.

In 1 Peter 3:7, Peter describes women as the weaker partner. However, modern times call for women to be a ruthless, independent businesswoman or a superwoman homeschool mom. The double standard is exhausting and causes us to avoid any appearance of weakness. We fear weakness—or at least I do.

 When weak, we feel we lack the strength to carry on. How else do you feel when you are weak?

 Have you ever felt strong when you were weak? How so or why not?

How is Paul able to make the statement that when he is weak, then he is strong? (Refer to 2 Corinthians 12:7-10.)

It seems totally backwards and counterintuitive. And yes, God's ways may seem backwards. "For the foolishness of God is wiser than human wisdom, and the weakness of God is stronger than human strength" (I Cor. 1:25). And the best part? We have access to that strength!

Whether you quote it or look it up, write out Philippians 4:13 and underline the source of our strength.

Finally, it is God's limitless strength that renews us at his right hand! Look at how Isaiah 40:28-31 emphasizes this strength:

Do you not know?
Have you not heard?
The Lord is the everlasting God,
the Creator of the ends of the earth.
He will not grow tired or weary,
and his understanding no one can fathom.
He gives strength to the weary
and increases the power of the weak.
Even youths grow tired and weary,
and young men stumble and fall;
but those who hope in the Lord
will renew their strength.
They will soar on wings like eagles;
they will run and not grow weary,
they will walk and not be faint.

We all long to be lifted up when we are down, strengthened when we are weak, comforted when we are hurting. God's right hand is the ultimate source of that strength. As you look to the Common Threads, think about God turning one of your thorns—a weakness—into strength!

Also, in the same way that Barnabas, the son of encouragement, and Paul were extended the right hand of fellowship by James, Cephas, and John (Gal. 2:9), may you and your Iron Rose Sisters be embraced by the strengthening right hand of fellowship and en-couragement you can provide each other.

Common Threads:

An area in which you'd like to grow or bloom.

_____

_____

A thorn you'd like to remove.

_____

_____

An area in which you'd like to dig deeper or need someone to hold you accountable.

_____

_____

A message of hope, an encouraging word, or scripture.

CHAPTER 5

A Standard of Righteousness

People-watching is one of my favorite hobbies. Airports are one of the best places to observe people's interactions: a grandma's first time to meet the new baby, a soldier home from war greeted by his family, a tearful farewell, the businesswoman ready to kick off her heels as soon as she gets home...

The beach is another entertaining place to watch people. No, I'm not referring to the scantily clad young women or muscle-bound men. I much prefer scanning the beach for a young family. My search is for a young child who jumps to try and reach the footprints his dad has left in the sand. He wants to measure up to his daddy. His longing to be a "big boy" and the strong example his dad has provided are all wrapped up in the leap from one footprint to the next.

The dad has left his mark, and while it may take a few years for the young boy to reach his goal, the standard has been established.

A standard is something by which all other things are measured. As women, we easily fall into the trap of comparison and may often feel that we do not measure up. When we look to God's teaching about righteousness, we may feel even more overwhelmed by *his* standards.

The Chinese character for righteousness is composed of two separate characters: one standing for a lamb, the other for "me." When "lamb" is placed directly above "me," a new character—"righteousness"—is formed. What an elegant visual representation of our righteousness before the Father!

"The next day John saw Jesus coming toward him and said, "Look, the Lamb of God, who takes away the sin of the world!" (John 1:29)

"God made him who had no sin to be sin for us, so that in him we might become the righteousness of God" (2 Cor. 5:21).

How would you define righteousness?

In brief, we will consider righteousness as being made right in God's eyes, as well as right living after having been made right.

"Shall I go on sinning so that grace may increase? By no means!" (Rom. 6:1) After being blessed so greatly by being made right with God, our response is one of humble gratitude. Our obedience is a byproduct of our thanksgiving and a sign of submission to the authority of God's right hand.

What is God's right hand filled with? (Ps. 48:10)

My Fear of God's Righteous Right Hand

When I was studying the Bible in order to become a Christian, my biggest hindrance was my fear that I would not measure up. I understood God's standard of righteousness all too well. Growing up in a Christian home, the teachings of Scripture and the call to obedience were clear. This oldest child with a people-pleaser personality worked hard to earn her parents' approval. Wasn't that also how it worked with God? Didn't I have to earn my salvation and be a "good enough" example to others?

My sister, Jenn, who is three years younger than me, was also studying the Bible around the same time. We were both studying about how to become a Christian and what it meant to be one.

One Wednesday before evening church services, my sister told my parents that she was ready to be baptized. I overheard the conversation from another part of the house and was shocked. In reality, indignant, angry, and confused might more accurately have described my reaction.

I was the older sister! I knew more Bible verses than her! I was more obedient—the much better child (yes, pride was definitely on my list of faults)! I did not understand what my younger sister, at age ten, knew that I didn't at age thirteen.

And then it hit me. It wasn't about what she knew or about what she did. It wasn't about what I knew or what I did. It was about what God had done by sacrificing his Son as a perfect atonement for our sins—nothing we could earn, but a free gift—by grace.

"For it is by grace you have been saved, through faith—and this is not from yourselves, it is the gift of God—not by works, so that no one can boast" (Eph. 2:8-9).

That night, my sister's decision was the wake-up call that opened my eyes to the significance of grace. And so, a few hours later on March 20, 1991, my dad baptized me, and then my sister, for the remission of sins and that we might receive the gift of the Holy Spirit (Acts 2:38).

My limited perspective had me focused on a fear of judgment at God's righteous right hand. I had not yet tasted the promises and blessings at "his righteous right hand" in Isaiah 41:10, and the other characteristics we have studied thus far.

I forgot that it was not Abraham's righteous acts, but rather his faith, that was credited to him as righteousness (Gen. 15:6; Rom. 4:22). I fell into the same pitfall as the Israelites.

 What was that pitfall according to Romans 10:3?

We must submit to God's righteousness *and* his guidance!

Guided Teaching in God's Right Hand

I grew up in the kitchen. All four of us girls did. And now we all enjoy cooking as adults. As a baby, some of my nephew's favorite toys were a pot and spoon. As he has gotten a little older, an empty pot is insufficient. He wants to be more hands-on, cooking with us.

Thankfully, cooking was modeled in such a way that we learned hand-in-hand with my mom and have been able to pass those skills on to others. Parental guidance is important at all stages of life. I vividly remember my tiny right hand enveloped by my mom's larger right hand on the handheld mixer, making some of my favorites—zucchini bread, banana cookies, or snicker-doodles.

With her left hand holding the bowl and her right hand guiding mine, there was no guarantee that I would not still manage to make a mess of things, but I knew I wasn't alone.

Just as a loving parent would, God takes our right hand in his and guides us through the learning process of life. And if we make a mess of things, he's right there with us to clean it up.

I am a fiercely independent person. I like to think I know what I'm doing, am highly capable, and clear on the path I should take. When I reject the guidance of God's right hand, I pay the price. I receive loving discipline and suffer the consequences of my actions, words, and decisions.

Guided to Righteousness through Discipline

"This hurts me more than it hurts you." I never understood why my dad said that before disciplining us as children. Discipline is not fun for the giver or the receiver. But as I've matured, I have begun to understand the perspective of the one giving the discipline just a little bit more.

I have had dreams in which my arm became paralyzed and I was physically unable to spank my nephew or someone else in need of a physical reminder of the consequences of disobedience. (The dream may be premature since my nephew is at an age when time out is still an effective form of discipline.) However, I believe the dream represented my hesitancy due to my distaste for discipline.

 What does Hebrews 12:4-11 say about discipline and the harvest it produces?

 Why does God discipline us?

Why do we require discipline?

Discipline is one of the direct consequences of disobedience. What is obedience a direct result of? Love.

Read John 14:23-27. What is promised to those who love Christ and obey his commands?

Are we left alone to figure out what to obey? Who guides us?

 How does the guidance come?

 What good is the guidance if we don't follow it?

 We avoid God's guidance and teaching, not because we don't believe it, but because we *do* believe it. Do you agree with that statement? Why or why not?

Lost and confused, we reject God's right hand of discipline and avoid his hand of guidance (Ps. 139:10) even though it is precisely what we need.

Guided in Paths of Righteousness

"And his commands are not burdensome" (1 John 5:3b). Rather, they are designed to protect and guide me in paths of righteousness.

 What is the imagery of God's guidance in Psalm 23?

Where does he lead us (Ps. 23:3)?

According to Psalm 23, what is God's purpose in guiding us?

 Why do we resist being led in the path of righteousness?

The path of righteousness can be scary if we don't trust the one whose hand we hold. We think it is better to stay "safe," comfortable, or stagnant than to embrace the One who is good, the One whose standard is righteousness. As a loving Father, he wants what is best for us. As our Creator, he also truly *knows* what is best, good, and right for his creation. So why do we fear him and his ways?

C.S. Lewis describes the scary feelings we might face when confronted by the King in an allegory in the seven-title series *The Chronicles of Narnia*. In *The Lion, the Witch, and the Wardrobe*, God is compared to the lion, Aslan, who Mr. and Mrs. Beaver describe to Susan and Lucy:

"You'll understand when you see him."

"But shall we see him?" asked Susan.

"Why, Daughter of Eve, that's what I brought you here for. I'm to lead you to where you shall meet him," said Mr. Beaver.

"Is—is he a man?" asked Lucy.

"Aslan a man!" said Mr. Beaver sternly. "Certainly not. I tell you he is the King of the wood and the son of the great Emperor-beyond-the-Sea. Don't you know who is the King of beasts? Aslan is a lion—the Lion, the great Lion."

"Ooh!" said Susan, "I'd thought he was a man. Is he—quite safe? I shall feel rather nervous about meeting a lion."

"That you will, dearie, and no mistake," said Mrs. Beaver; "if there's anyone who can appear before Aslan without their knees knocking, they're either braver than most or else just silly."

"Then he isn't safe?" said Lucy.

"Safe?" said Mr. Beaver; "don't you hear what Mrs. Beaver tells you? Who said anything about safe? 'Course he isn't safe. But he's good. He's the King, I tell you."

 What is the difference between safe and good?

Which is the more vital characteristic for the King of kings? Why?

 Why is it important for God to be good?

Use the following verses to answer the question: How does God guide us in his good and right ways?

Romans 12:2

Colossians 1:9

"But seek first his kingdom and his righteousness, and all these things will be given to you as well" (Matt. 6:33).

What do Romans 14:17-18 and I Timothy 6:11 tell us are the most important things?

 Give four ways we can put those things into action this week.

How does Romans 8:9-17 describe the righteous life?

What does Paul contrast with being a slave to fear in Romans 8:15-17?

As God's children and co-heirs with Christ, we are among the righteous who can proclaim victory! (See Psalm 118:15-19 below.)

Shouts of joy and victory
resound in the tents of the righteous:
"The Lord's right hand has done mighty things!
The Lord's right hand is lifted high;
the Lord's right hand has done mighty things!"
I will not die but live,
and will proclaim what the Lord has done.
The Lord has chastened me severely,
but he has not given me over to death.
Open for me the gates of the righteous;
I will enter and give thanks to the Lord.
This is the gate of the Lord
through which the righteous may enter.
I will give you thanks, for you answered me;
you have become my salvation.

We can enter through the righteous gates with confidence, free of fear, cleansed of a guilty conscience because of Christ's sacrifice, once and for all!

Read Hebrews 10:19-25 as an affirmation of this confidence, a final activity for this chapter, and a timely transition to our last chapter "Where Jesus Sits to

Intercede." Before we close, let's put verses 23-25 into practice through the Common Threads!

Common Threads:

An area in which you'd like to grow or bloom.

_____

_____

A thorn you'd like to remove.

_____

_____

An area in which you'd like to dig deeper or need someone to hold you accountable.

_____

_____

A message of hope, an encouraging word, or scripture.

_____

_____

CHAPTER 6

Where Jesus Sits to Intercede

Tim Rohn, an inspirational speaker, says, "You are the average of the five people you spend the most time with." Make a list of the five people you spend the most time with. This may include your spouse, your kids, coworkers, roommates, or friends.

 Do you agree that you are the average of those people, for better or worse? Why or why not?

Those with whom we spend the most time greatly influence the way in which we live our lives, make decisions, speak, act, and react. They are the first ones we call or text with good news. They are the ones we know we can count on through the tough times.

This is especially true of those people we choose to have at our right hand. It is a place of honor in our own lives that comes with great responsibility.

Name two people who have greatly influenced your life—positively or negatively.

We have a choice about whom we allow at our right hand and the power we give them.

Who is at Joshua's right hand in Zechariah 3:1? What is he doing?

 Ever feel like Satan is at your right hand accusing your every move? What can we do about that?

Jesus Intercedes at God's Right Hand

Among the many words of hope that Peter offers the crowd on the Day of Pentecost, what promise from David does he quote in Acts 2:25?

So, if Satan is at our right hand to accuse, but Jesus is also there at our right hand, what will be the outcome of that battle—every time?

In Acts 2:34, Peter quotes the prophecy found in Psalm 110:1 and describes the outcome of that battle. (This same prophecy is also in Matthew 22:44, Mark 12:36, and Luke 20:42.)

The Lord says to my Lord:
"Sit at my right hand
until I make your enemies
a footstool for your feet."

Where is Jesus now (Acts 2:33-34)?

 What do you think it means to make your enemies a footstool for your feet?

Jesus is the culmination and embodiment of all of the promises and blessings at God's right hand. He is the personification of each of the facets of God's right hand that we have explored up to this point.

And as the central figure of the entire story of the Bible, it is fitting that Jesus be the central figure at God's right hand. Therefore, in this final chapter, we will rediscover Jesus as the manifestation of the five descriptions of God's right hand that we have investigated thus far.

A Place of Honor and Blessing—Seated at God's Right Hand

Just as Jacob blessed Joseph's sons with a place of honor in the family at his right hand, Jesus sits at God's right hand (Matt. 26:64; Mark 14:62, 16:19; and Luke 22:69)—the ultimate place of honor, which is the seat of blessing for us (Eph. 2:6).

Can we sit at a place of honor and blessing without Christ?

Fill in the blank below using John 1:12-13 and Galatians 3:26-27 as inspiration.

 Adoption as daughters of the King is _____ because of Jesus' sacrifice.

What else do the above verses highlight?

Jesus, the Promise of Protection and Salvation

A child may be scared of the dark or fear the monster under the bed. When afraid, she goes to her parents for love, comfort, and protection. The security she finds in their arms is the kind of security we long for and can only receive in the arms of our loving heavenly Father.

 What protection does Jesus offer women today? How does he help you face your deepest fears?

From what else do we specifically need Jesus' protection and salvation (Rom. 3:10, 23, and 6:23)?

 Based on Romans 8:34, what does Jesus protect us from?

Write out Romans 8:1 as an echo of that sentiment.

Only Jesus' perfect sacrifice made true protection and ultimate salvation possible (Heb. 1:3, 10:12, and 12:2). In each of the three aforementioned verses, we see that after Jesus completed his work, he sat at the right hand of God. It was only after he had done his work, making it possible for us to join him at God's right hand, that he sat there to rest and extend the invitation.

Jesus Exercises Power and Authority

In the Old Testament, God showed his authority by spreading out the heavens, shattering enemies, and displaying victorious power. And in the New Testament, we see additional demonstrations of power and authority. What things does Jesus have authority over in the following stories?

Matthew 9:1-8

Mark 4:35-41

Luke 4:31-37

John 9:1-12

John 11:17-44

Jesus had power and authority over nature, demons, and even death!

 How does he exercise that power and authority today?

 What did Jesus do just before he ascended with the authority given to him (Matt. 28:18-20)?

An Example and Source of Strength

The early church, whose history we have in the book of Acts and in the church today, have been called to maintain Christ as the head of his body (Eph.

1:18-23 and 4:15). However, the authority under which the church functions is also the love under which we are protected and strengthened (Eph. 5:23-32).

We see examples throughout the book of Acts in which many of the early followers of "the Way" (Acts 9:2), kept their eyes fixed on Jesus, the head of the church *and* their individual lives, as their source of strength. For example, Acts 7 retells the story of Stephen's speech to the Sanhedrin. Verses 51-53 give a summary of his sermon, and then we see what happened next. Read Acts 7:51-60.

What did Stephen see when he looked up to heaven?

What strength did Stephen rely on?

What were Jesus' sources of strength while in the Garden of Gethsemane (Matt. 26:36-46)?

Just as Jesus could not face that difficult time alone, we can follow his example of looking to the Father, praying, seeking the support of friends, and relying on the Holy Spirit (Acts 2:33). Christ's very example is a source of strength (Phil. 4:13).

In Jesus, We Are the Righteousness of God

And through Christ's commitment to fulfilling God's will as the perfect sacrifice, "he who had no sin [became] sin so that we might become the righteousness of God" (2 Cor. 5:21).

 Now that Jesus has provided the way (John 14:6), what do the verses in Acts 5:31-32 and Colossians 3:1 say is our continued responsibility for righteous living?

 What is the underlying motivation for Christ—and for us—to obey? (John 15:9-17)

Protection from Fear in Christ

John, known as the apostle that Jesus loved, paints many pictures of God's love in his gospel and the book of 1 John. He describes perfect love in 1 John 4:7-20. How do we know that it's perfect love? Because God is love! (1 John 4:8 and 16)

 Read 1 John 4:13-18. What does perfect love do and how does it do it?

If we dwell in God's love, truly whom shall we fear?

"Fear can keep you up all night, but faith makes one fine pillow."
~ Anonymous (Ref. Matt. 21:21-22)

Reflecting on God's Right Hand

 Which facet of God's right hand is most encouraging to you at this point in your life? Why that characteristic?

_____ A place of honor and blessing

_____ A promise of protection and salvation

_____ A demonstration of power and authority

_____ A source of strength

_____ A standard of righteousness

_____ Where Jesus sits to intercede

 Which facet of God's right hand best reminds you that you have nothing to fear? Why that characteristic?

 How has the reminder of these descriptions of God's character shaped or deepened your relationship with him?

Seated at God's right hand, Jesus sits in the place of honor to intercede for us. Without him, there is no promise of protection or salvation. When we allow Jesus to demonstrate his power and authority in the church and in our individual lives, we rely on him as our source of strength and an example of how we can live a righteous life. And the best part? Through Christ, we have become the righteousness of God (2 Cor. 5:21) and need not fear because of the Father's perfect love.

Common Threads:

An area in which you'd like to grow or bloom.

_____

_____

A thorn you'd like to remove.

_____

_____

An area in which you'd like to dig deeper or need someone to hold you accountable.

_____

_____

A message of hope, an encouraging word, or scripture.

_____

_____

Closing Remarks

Thank you for joining hands with the Father and with one another in knowing God more intimately through a study of his right hand.

As daughters of the King, securely upheld in his right hand, whom shall we fear? Nothing! Affirmed through a vivid description of our heavenly Father that transcends the Old and New Testament, God's right hand is a special place of honor from which he demonstrates power and authority, promises protection and salvation, and provides a source of strength. God's righteous right hand is also where Jesus sits to intercede for us!

These are truths on which we can rely! His right hand is where we can securely rest, peaceful in the protection he provides, free of fear, and filled with hope.

With only one minor edit, I want to share the following song with you that I wrote my senior year of college. It is my prayerful invitation to join hands together with God and one another as we continue on the journey.

God's Right Hand We Hold

Will you think and pray for me
As I think and pray for you?
While we're apart in time and space
It's all that we can do.

Chorus:
Our lives are held in God's hands,
He is in control.
When so many things tear us away,
God's right hand we hold.

We both call God our Father,
Our bond is more than friends.
And through the blood of Jesus,
The friendship never ends.

Notes

_____

_____

_____

_____

_____

_____

_____

_____

_____

_____

_____

_____

_____

_____

_____

_____

_____

_____

_____

About the Author

Michelle J. Goff has been writing small group Bible study materials in English and in Spanish throughout her ministry career. God has led Michelle to share these resources with more women across the world through Iron Rose Sister Ministries, a registered non-profit. She also continues to take advantage of opportunities for speaking engagements, seminars, women's retreats, and other women's ministry events across the Americas, in both English and in Spanish. If you would like to book a seminar in your area, please contact Michelle at ironrosesister@gmail.com, or for more information, visit www.IronRoseSister.com.

Personal Life

Michelle grew up in Baton Rouge, Louisiana, with her parents and three younger sisters. Her love and desire for helping women in their journey began early with her sisters, even when they thought she was being bossy. They've all grown a lot from those early years, but the sisterly bonds remain. Michelle has been blessed by the support of her family through all of her endeavors over the years.

Michelle enjoys time with family, cheering on the Atlanta Braves and the Louisiana State University Tigers, having coffee with friends, movies, travel, and speaking Spanish. And guess what her favorite flower is? Yep. The red rose.

She currently resides in Searcy, Arkansas, near her parents.

Ministry and Educational Experience

Michelle first felt called into ministry during her senior year at Harding University while obtaining a Bachelor of Arts degree in Communication Disorders and Spanish. She planned to join a team to plant a church in north

Bogotá, Colombia, so she moved to Atlanta after graduating in May 1999 to facilitate that church-plant. Even though the plan for a Bogotá team fell through, Michelle continued her dream to be a part of a church plant there, which happened in March 2000.

She worked in the missions ministry at the North Atlanta Church of Christ for eighteen months before moving to Denver to work with English- and Spanish-speaking church plants there (Highlands Ranch Church of Christ and three Spanish-speaking congregations). During her two-and-a-half years there, Michelle continued her involvement in Bogotá and throughout various regions of Venezuela, visiting new church plants, teaching classes, conducting women's retreats, and speaking at and volunteering with youth camps.

In March 2003, Michelle moved to Caracas, Venezuela, to assist with a church planting on the eastern side of the city. Her time in Caracas was focused on the East Caracas congregation, but she was also able to participate in other women's activities across the country. In the four years Michelle spent in Caracas, the congregation grew from the twelve people meeting in her apartment to almost 100 meeting in a hotel conference room. The East Caracas congregation recently celebrated its twelfth anniversary and is still going strong. A visit to Bogotá every three months to renew her Venezuelan visa also facilitated continued assistance with the congregation there.

In March 2007, Michelle transitioned back into ministry in the United States as the women's campus minister for the South Baton Rouge Church of Christ at the Christian Student Center (CSC) near the LSU campus. While walking with the college students on their spiritual journey and serving in other women's ministry roles, Michelle also pursued her "nerdy passion" of Spanish. She graduated from LSU in December 2011 with a Masters in Hispanic Studies, Linguistics Concentration. Her thesis explored the influence of social and religious factors in the interpretation of Scripture.

Michelle is now following God's calling to use her bilingual ministry experience with women of all ages and cultural backgrounds to bless them with opportunities for growth and deep spiritual connection with other Christian sisters through Iron Rose Sister Ministries.

About Iron Rose Sister Ministries

Vision:

To equip women to connect to God and one another more deeply.

Iron Rose Sister Ministries

Ministerio Hermana Rosa de Hierro

www.IronRoseSister.com

Overall Mission:

A ministry that facilitates Christian sister relationships that will be like iron sharpening iron, encouraging and inspiring each other to be as beautiful as a rose in spite of a few thorns. Its goal is to provide women's Bible studies that are simple enough for anyone to lead and yet, deep enough for everyone to grow. These resources are available in English and Spanish (Iron Rose Sister Ministries - IRSM / Ministerio Hermana Rosa de Hierro - MHRH).

FACETS of Iron Rose Sister Ministries' vision:

F – Faithfulness – to God above all else. First and foremost: *"Seek first His kingdom and His righteousness and all these things will be added to you as well"(Matt. 6:33).*

A – Authenticity – We're not hypocrites, just human. *"But he said to me, "My grace is sufficient for you, for my power is made perfect in weakness." Therefore I will boast all the more gladly about my weaknesses, so that Christ's power may rest on me. That is why, for Christ's sake, I delight in weaknesses, in insults, in hardships, in persecutions, in difficulties. For when I am weak, then I am strong"(2 Cor. 12:9-10).*

C – Community – We were not created to have an isolated relationship with God. He has designed the church as a body with many parts (*1 Cor. 12*). The magnitude of "one another" passages in the New Testament affirms this design. As women, we have unique relational needs at various stages in life—whether we are going through a time in which we need, like Moses, our arms raised in support by others (*Ex. 17:12*) or are able to rejoice with those who rejoice and mourn with those who mourn (*Rom. 12:15*). The Iron Rose Sister Ministries studies are designed to be shared in community.

E – Encouragement through Prayer and Accountability – *"As iron sharpens iron, so one person sharpens another"(Prov. 27:17).* God has not left us alone in this journey. *"Confess your sins to each other and pray for each other so that you may be healed. The prayer of a righteous man is powerful and effective"(James 5:16).* It is our prayer that every woman that joins in this mission participates as an Iron Rose Sister with other women, partnering in prayer and loving accountability.

T – Testimony – We all have a "God story." By recognizing his living and active hand in our lives, we are blessed to share that message of hope with others (*John 4:39-42*). Thankfully, that story is not over! God continues to work in the transformation of lives, and we long to hear your story.

S – Study – *"The Word of God is alive and active. Sharper than any double-edged sword, it penetrates even to dividing soul and spirit, joints and marrow; it judges the thoughts and attitudes of the heart"* (*Heb. 4:12*).

In order to fully realize the blessing, benefit, and design of the Iron Rose Sister Ministries vision, we must go to the Creator. Through a greater knowledge of the Word, we can blossom as roses and remove a few thorns— discerning the leading of the Spirit, recognizing the voice of the Father, and following the example of the Son. This is more effectively accomplished in community (small group Bible studies), but not to the exclusion of time alone with God (personal Bible study).

For more information, please:

Visit www.IronRoseSister.com.

Sign up for the IRSM daily blog and monthly newsletter.

IRSM is a registered 501(c)(3) public nonprofit with a board of directors and advisory eldership.

References to God's Right Hand in the Bible

Exodus 15:6: Your **right hand**, Lord, was majestic in power. Your **right hand**, Lord, shattered the enemy.

Exodus 15:12: You stretch out your **right hand**, and the earth swallows your enemies.

Psalm 16:11: You make known to me the path of life; you will fill me with joy in your presence, with eternal pleasures at your **right hand**.

Psalm 17:7: Show me the wonders of your great love, you who save by your **right hand** those who take refuge in you from their foes.

Psalm 18:35: You make your saving help my shield, and your **right hand** sustains me; your help has made me great.

Psalm 20:6: Now this I know: The Lord gives victory to his anointed. He answers him from his heavenly sanctuary with the victorious power of his **right hand**.

Psalm 21:8: Your hand will lay hold on all your enemies; your **right hand** will seize your foes.

Psalm 44:3: It was not by their sword that they won the land, nor did their arm bring them victory; it was your **right hand**, your arm, and the light of your face, for you loved them.

Psalm 45:4: In your majesty ride forth victoriously in the cause of truth, humility and justice; let your **right hand** achieve awesome deeds.

Psalm 48:10: Like your name, O God, your praise reaches to the ends of the earth; your **right hand** is filled with righteousness.

Psalm 60:5: Save us and help us with your **right hand**, that those you love may be delivered.

Psalm 63:8: I cling to you; your **right hand** upholds me.

Psalm 74:11: Why do you hold back your hand, your **right hand**? Take it from the folds of your garment and destroy them!

Psalm 77:10: Then I thought, "To this I will appeal: the years when the Most High stretched out his **right hand**."

Psalm 78:54: And so he brought them to the border of his holy land, to the hill country his **right hand** had taken.

Psalm 80:15: ...the root your **right hand** has planted, the son you have raised up for yourself.

Psalm 80:17: Let your hand rest on the man at your **right hand**, the son of man you have raised up for yourself.

Psalm 89:13: Your arm is endowed with power; your hand is strong, your **right hand** exalted.

Psalm 98:1: Sing to the Lord a new song, for he has done marvelous things; his **right hand** and his holy arm have worked salvation for him.

Psalm 108:6: Save us and help us with your **right hand**, that those you love may be delivered.

Psalm 109:31: For he stands at the **right hand** of the needy, to save their lives from those who would condemn them.

Psalm 110:1: The Lord says to my lord: "Sit at my **right hand** until I make your enemies a footstool for your feet."

Psalm 118:15: Shouts of joy and victory resound in the tents of the righteous: "The Lord's **right hand** has done mighty things!"

Psalm 118:16: "The Lord's **right hand** is lifted high; the Lord's **right hand** has done mighty things!"

Psalm 138:7: Though I walk in the midst of trouble, you preserve my life. You stretch out your hand against the anger of my foes; with your **right hand** you save me.

Psalm 139:10: ...even there your hand will guide me, your **right hand** will hold me fast.

Isaiah 41:10: So do not fear, for I am with you; do not be dismayed, for I am your God. I will strengthen you and help you; I will uphold you with my righteous **right hand**.

Isaiah 48:13: My own hand laid the foundations of the earth, and my **right hand** spread out the heavens; when I summon them, they all stand up together.

Isaiah 62:8: The Lord has sworn by his **right hand** and by his mighty arm: "Never again will I give your grain as food for your enemies, and never again will foreigners drink the new wine for which you have toiled..."

Jeremiah 22:24: "As surely as I live," declares the Lord, "even if you, Jehoiachin son of Jehoiakim king of Judah, were a signet ring on my **right hand**, I would still pull you off."

Lamentations 2:3: In fierce anger he has cut off every horn of Israel. He has withdrawn his **right hand** at the approach of the enemy. He has burned in Jacob like a flaming fire that consumes everything around it.

Lamentations 2:4: Like an enemy he has strung his bow; his **right hand** is ready. Like a foe he has slain all who were pleasing to the eye; he has poured out his wrath like fire on the tent of Daughter Zion.

Ezekiel 21:22: Into his **right hand** will come the lot for Jerusalem, where he is to set up battering rams, to give the command to slaughter, to sound the battle cry, to set battering rams against the gates, to build a ramp and to erect siege works.

Habakkuk 2:16: You will be filled with shame instead of glory. Now it is your turn! Drink and let your nakedness be exposed! The cup from the Lord's **right hand** is coming around to you, and disgrace will cover your glory.

Matthew 22:44: "'The Lord said to my Lord: 'Sit at my **right hand** until I put your enemies under your feet.'"

Matthew 26:64: "You have said so," Jesus replied. "But I say to all of you: From now on you will see the Son of Man sitting at the **right hand** of the Mighty One and coming on the clouds of heaven."

Matthew 27:29: ...and then twisted together a crown of thorns and set it on his head. They put a staff in his **right hand**. Then they knelt in front of him and mocked him. "Hail, king of the Jews!" they said.

Mark 12:36: David himself, speaking by the Holy Spirit, declared: "'The Lord said to my Lord: 'Sit at my **right hand** until I put your enemies under your feet.'"

Mark 14:62: "I am," said Jesus. "And you will see the Son of Man sitting at the **right hand** of the Mighty One and coming on the clouds of heaven."

Mark 16:19: After the Lord Jesus had spoken to them, he was taken up into heaven and he sat at the **right hand** of God.

Luke 20:42: David himself declares in the Book of Psalms: "'The Lord said to my Lord: 'Sit at my **right hand**...'"

Luke 22:69: But from now on, the Son of Man will be seated at the **right hand** of the mighty God.

Acts 2:33: Exalted to the **right hand** of God, he has received from the Father the promised Holy Spirit and has poured out what you now see and hear.

Acts 2:34: For David did not ascend to heaven, and yet he said, "The Lord said to my Lord: 'Sit at my **right hand**...'"

Acts 5:31: God exalted him to his own **right hand** as Prince and Savior that he might bring Israel to repentance and forgive their sins.

Acts 7:55: But Stephen, full of the Holy Spirit, looked up to heaven and saw the glory of God, and Jesus standing at the **right hand** of God.

Acts 7:56: "Look," he said, "I see heaven open and the Son of Man standing at the **right hand** of God."

Romans 8:34: Who then is the one who condemns? No one. Christ Jesus who died—more than that, who was raised to life—is at the **right hand** of God and is also interceding for us.

Ephesians 1:20: ...he exerted when he raised Christ from the dead and seated him at his **right hand** in the heavenly realms...

Colossians 3:1: Since, then, you have been raised with Christ, set your hearts on things above, where Christ is, seated at the **right hand** of God.

Hebrews 1:3: The Son is the radiance of God's glory and the exact representation of his being, sustaining all things by his powerful word. After he had provided purification for sins, he sat down at the **right hand** of the Majesty in heaven.

Hebrews 1:13: To which of the angels did God ever say, "Sit at my **right hand** until I make your enemies a footstool for your feet"?

Hebrews 8:1: Now the main point of what we are saying is this: We do have such a high priest, who sat down at the **right hand** of the throne of the Majesty in heaven...

Hebrews 10:12: But when this priest had offered for all time one sacrifice for sins, he sat down at the **right hand** of God,

Hebrews 12:2: ...fixing our eyes on Jesus, the pioneer and perfecter of faith. For the joy set before him he endured the cross, scorning its shame, and sat down at the **right hand** of the throne of God.

1 Peter 3:22: ...who has gone into heaven and is at God's **right hand**—with angels, authorities and powers in submission to him.

Revelation 1:16: In his **right hand** he held seven stars, and coming out of his mouth was a sharp, double-edged sword. His face was like the sun shining in all its brilliance.

Revelation 1:17: When I saw him, I fell at his feet as though dead. Then he placed his **right hand** on me and said: "Do not be afraid. I am the First and the Last."

Revelation 1:20: The mystery of the seven stars that you saw in my **right hand** and of the seven golden lampstands is this: The seven stars are the angels of the seven churches, and the seven lampstands are the seven churches.

Revelation 2:1: "To the angel of the church in Ephesus write: These are the words of him who holds the seven stars in his **right hand** and walks among the seven golden lampstands."

Revelation 5:1: Then I saw in the **right hand** of him who sat on the throne a scroll with writing on both sides and sealed with seven seals.

Revelation 5:7: He went and took the scroll from the **right hand** of him who sat on the throne.

References to God at Our Right Hand

Psalm 16:8: I keep my eyes always on the Lord. With him at my **right hand**, I will not be shaken.

Psalm 73:23: Yet I am always with you; you hold me by my **right hand**.

Psalm 110:5: The Lord is at your **right hand**; he will crush kings on the day of his wrath.

Psalm 121:5: The Lord watches over you— the Lord is your shade at your **right hand**...

Isaiah 41:13: For I am the Lord your God who takes hold of your **right hand** and says to you, Do not fear; I will help you.

Isaiah 63:12: ...who sent his glorious arm of power to be at Moses' **right hand**, who divided the waters before them, to gain for himself everlasting renown...

Acts 2:25: David said about him: "'I saw the Lord always before me. Because he is at my **right hand**, I will not be shaken."

Additional References to the Right Hand

Genesis 48:13: And Joseph took both of them, Ephraim on his right toward Israel's left hand and Manasseh on his left toward Israel's **right hand**, and brought them close to him.

Genesis 48:14: But Israel reached out his **right hand** and put it on Ephraim's head, though he was the younger, and crossing his arms, he put his left hand on Manasseh's head, even though Manasseh was the firstborn.

Genesis 48:17: When Joseph saw his father placing his **right hand** on Ephraim's head he was displeased; so he took hold of his father's hand to move it from Ephraim's head to Manasseh's head.

Genesis 48:18: Joseph said to him, "No, my father, this one is the firstborn; put your **right hand** on his head."

Psalm 91:7: A thousand may fall at your side, ten thousand at your **right hand**, but it will not come near you.

Daniel 12:7: The man clothed in linen, who was above the waters of the river, lifted his **right hand** and his left hand toward heaven, and I heard him swear by him who lives forever, saying, "It will be for a time, times and half a time. When the power of the holy people has been finally broken, all these things will be completed."

Matthew 5:30: And if your **right hand** causes you to stumble, cut it off and throw it away. It is better for you to lose one part of your body than for your whole body to go into hell.

Galatians 2:9: James, Cephas and John, those esteemed as pillars, gave me and Barnabas the **right hand** of fellowship when they recognized the grace given to me. They agreed that we should go to the Gentiles, and they to the circumcised.

Revelation 10:5: Then the angel I had seen standing on the sea and on the land raised his **right hand** to heaven.

Made in the USA
Charleston, SC
01 August 2015